CONTENTS

PREFACE

Singing songs of praise, happiness, and love—for Jesus, for God, and for each other, is a privilege we need to share with the youngest child. But that sharing must be on his or her level, not on ours. *Songs for Preschool Children* has been compiled with this purpose in mind.

Because preschool children think in literal terms, we have avoided symbolism. "Tell it like it is" is a good motto to remember when working with young children.

Our songs are purposely kept short, with as simple a melody line as possible. They range, for the most part, from middle C to the C above it because this is where young children sing.

The vocabulary is simple so that the message of the songs will be understandable to the children.

Preschoolers have a short attention span and need a change of pace from time to time. Make use of the action songs to allow the children time to stretch and relax their muscles. They'll be more attentive to the story, or whatever comes next, if they have had an opportunity to unwind—physically and mentally.

Songs present an effective means of helping children remember. Scriptures put to music will quickly become a part of a child's repertoire and will remain with him for years to come. Songs can be used to give simple commands. Singing "Put the toys away" is far more effective than telling the children to pick up and get ready for more serious business. Put music to work for you throughout your program or your day.

To make this book practical for busy parents, teachers, and song leaders, we have arranged the songs in categories that are within the preschool child's understanding. Look for songs with a message that will reinforce the concepts being taught your child, your class, or group. Make your time of singing meaningful and happy. If you sing with enthuslasm and understanding, obviously enjoying this special time, the children will reflect those same attitudes.

On the index page are suggested ages for which the songs are best suited. Use songs that fit the needs, abilities, interests, and understanding of your children. By making music an important part of the life of each preschooler, he will be able to say with David, "I will sing unto the Lord as long as I live" (Psalm 104:33).

—Marian Bennett

Songs for Preschool Children

for ages
one
through
five

compiled by

MARIAN BENNETT

STANDARD PUBLISHING
Cincinnati, Ohio   5754

Library of Congress Cataloging in Publication Data

Bennett, Marian.
    Songs for preschool children.
        1. Children's songs. [1. Songs. 2. Hymns]
    1. Title
    M2193.S6949   783.6'75   80-25091
    ISBN 0-87239-429-8

ACTION SONG

E. P.

Eleanor Pankow

Additional suggestions: *Wave your arms. Blink your eyes. Tap your toes.*

HEADS AND SHOULDERS

(Tune: "Here We Go 'Round the Mulberry Bush")

Our heads, our shoulders, our knees, our toes;
Our heads, our shoulders, our knees, our toes;
Our heads, our shoulders, our knees, our toes;
We'll clap hands* together.

Turn around, stamp feet, bend over, wave arms, sit down, etc.

THE DO-RIGHT BUS

D. C.

Dot Cachiaras
Arr. by Michelle Pittinger

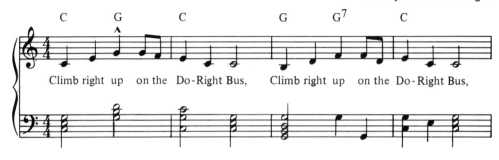

Climb right up on the Do-Right Bus, Climb right up on the Do-Right Bus,

Climb right up on the Do-Right Bus, and come a-long with us!

Make "stepping-up" motions with feet.

2. "Oom—oom—oom" goes the Do-Right Bus,
"Oom—oom—oom" goes the Do-Right Bus,
"Oom—oom—oom" goes the Do-Right Bus,
So come along with us!
(Make "motor sounds.")

3. Steer—steer—steer on the Do-Right Bus,
Steer—steer—steer on the Do-Right Bus,
Steer—steer—steer on the Do-Right Bus,
So come along with us!
(Pretend to hold steering wheel and steer.)

4. Up—the—hill goes the Do-Right Bus,
Up—the—hill goes the Do-Right Bus,
Up—the—hill goes the Do-Right Bus,
So come along with us!
(Hold pretend steering wheel higher.)

5. Down—the—hill goes the Do-Right Bus,
Down—the—hill goes the Do-Right Bus,
Down—the—hill goes the Do-Right Bus,
So come along with us!
(Lower pretend steering wheel.)

6. Doing right on the Do-Right Bus,
Doing right on the Do-Right Bus,
Doing right on the Do-Right Bus,
I'll do what's right, I must!
(Point to self and nod head.)

(To be sung when about to open the Do-Right Surprise Box.)
Peek inside of the Do-Right Bus,
Peek inside of the Do-Right Bus,
Peek inside of the Do-Right Bus,
And see what we can find!

I'M PRETTY SURE I KNOW

D. C.

Dot Cachiaras
Arr. by Michelle Pittinger

How man-y fin-gers? Snap, snap-py fin-gers? I'm pret-ty sure I know!
(1) (2) (3)

Ten snap-py fin-gers, snap, snap-py fin-gers, I'm pret-ty sure I know!
(1) (2) (3)

1. Hold up fingers. 2. Snap fingers. 3. Nod head.

2. How many shoulders? *(Hands on shoulders.)*
Tap-tappy shoulders? *(Tap shoulders.)*
I'm pretty sure I know! *(Nod head.)*
Two tappy shoulders, *(Hold up two fingers.)*
Tap-tappy shoulders, *(Tap shoulders.)*
I'm pretty sure I know! *(Nod head.)*

3. How many toeses? *(Point to toes.)*
Tip-tippy toeses? *(Walk on tiptoes.)*
I'm pretty sure I know! *(Nod head.)*
Ten-tippy toeses, *(Hold up ten fingers.)*
Tip-tippy toeses, *(Walk on tiptoes.)*
I'm pretty sure I know! *(Nod head.)*

4. How many noses? *(Point to nose.)*
Wig-wiggly noses? *(Wiggle nose.)*
I'm pretty sure I know! *(Nod head.)*
One wiggly nose, *(Hold up one finger.)*
Wig-wiggly nose, *(Wiggle nose.)*
I'm pretty sure I know! *(Nod head.)*

5. How many kneeses? *(Touch knees.)*
Bend-bendy kneeses? *(Bend knees.)*
I'm pretty sure I know! *(Nod head.)*
Two bendy kneeses, *(Hold up two fingers.)*
Bend-bendy kneeses, *(Bend knees.)*
I'm pretty sure I know! *(Nod head.)*

6. How many clappers? *(Hold up hands.)*
Clap-clappy clappers? *(Clap hands.)*
I'm pretty sure I know! *(Nod head.)*
Two clappy clappers, *(Hold up two fingers.)*
Clap-clappy clappers, *(Clap hands.)*
I'm pretty sure I know! *(Nod head.)*

7. How many elbows? *(Stick out elbows.)*
Craze, crazy elbows? *(Touch elbows.)*
I'm pretty sure I know! *(Nod head.)*
Two crazy elbows, *(Hold up two fingers.)*
Craze, crazy elbows, *(Touch elbows.)*
I'm pretty sure I know! *(Nod head.)*

8. Thank You, dear Father, *(Fold hands to pray.)*
Dear heav'nly Father,
Ten fingers, toes, one nose, *(Wiggle fingers, rise up on toes, point to nose.)*
Two hands that clap-clap, *(Clap hands.)*
Shoulders to tap-tap, *(Tap shoulders.)*
Two knees and two elbows. *(Bend knees, touch elbows.)*

7

DOWN, DOWN, DOWN

S. T.

Sylvia Tester

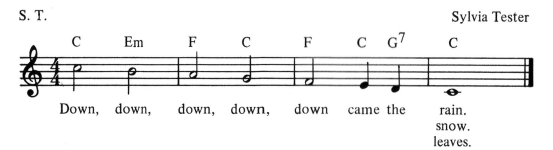

Down, down, down, down, down came the rain.
snow.
leaves.

ROLL THE BALL

S.T.

Sylvia Tester

Roll the ball to me. Roll the ball to you.
*Mary *Jane

Substitute other names.

I HAVE TWO HANDS

J.B.

Jean Baxendale
Arranged by Morine Barnes

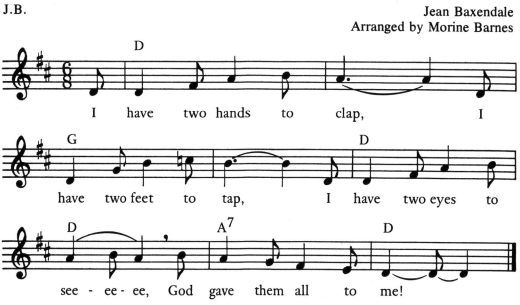

I have two hands to clap, I
have two feet to tap, I have two eyes to
see - ee - ee, God gave them all to me!

JINGLE, JINGLE, JOHNNY

E. P.

Eleanor Pankow

Jin - gle, jin - gle, John - ny,* Play a hap - py tune.

Play and skip, play and skip, All a - round the room.

Substitute children's names. Let children take turns skipping, running, hopping, jumping while playing rhythm instruments.

© 1981 by Eleanor Pankow. Used by permission.

LET'S PLAY WE ARE LITTLE BIRDS

M.A.

Mildred Adair

Let's play we are lit - tle birds,(1) Fly-ing,(2) fly-ing, fly - ing.___

Let's play we are lit - tle birds,___ Fly-ing, fly-ing fly - ing.___

1. dogs, bunnies; 2. running, hopping.

TIPTOE

M. A.

Mildred Adair

Tip - toe,* tip - toe, Light-ly now we're step - ping, Tip - toe, tip - toe,

Ev - 'ry step just so. Tip - toe, tip - toe,

With the mus-ic keep - ing, Tip - toe, tip - toe, Ev-'ry where we go.

*Marching

HERE'S A BLOCK

S.T.

Sylvia Tester

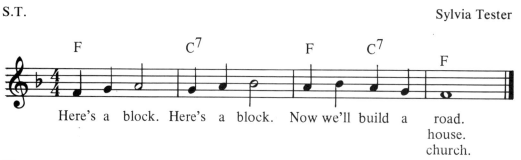

Here's a block. Here's a block. Now we'll build a road.
house.
church.

10

THE MARCHING SONG

D.F.R.

Dorothy Fay Richards

Marching, marching, here we go. Marching, marching,
(Walking, walking,)
here we go. Watch us proudly stepping,
ev-'ry step just so, just so. so, just so.

FAMILY FUN

J. B.

Jean Baxendale

Mom-my can jump, And I can too. Dad-dy can run, And I can too.

We jump and jump, And run and run. Our fam-i-ly has lots of fun!

Jump, jump, jump, jump, jump, jump, jump, jump! Sit down!
Run, run, run, run, run, run, run, run!

I'M SO HAPPY TODAY

D.F.R.

Dorothy Fay Richards

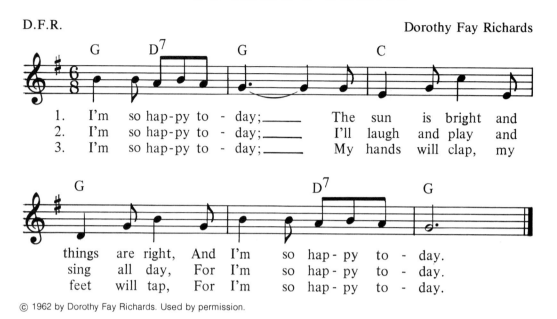

1. I'm so hap-py to - day;_____ The sun is bright and
2. I'm so hap-py to - day;_____ I'll laugh and play and
3. I'm so hap-py to - day;_____ My hands will clap, my

things are right, And I'm so hap - py to - day.
sing all day, For I'm so hap - py to - day.
feet will tap, For I'm so hap - py to - day.

ROCK THE BABY

S.T.

Sylvia Tester

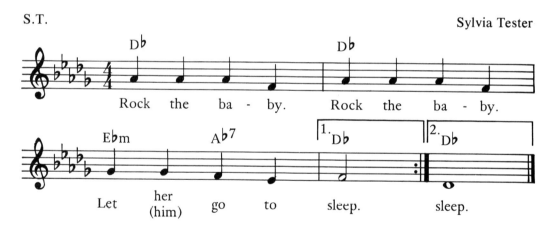

Rock the ba - by. Rock the ba - by.

Let her go to sleep. sleep.
(him)

TAKE MY HAND

S.T.

Sylvia Tester

Take my hand and walk with me. Take my hand and walk with me.

CLAP-TAP

M. H. F.

Marie H. Frost

Let's ev-'ry-one clap hands with me. *(clap, clap)* Let's

ev-'ry-one tap feet with me, *(tap, tap)* Make

hands go *(clap, clap)*, and make feet go *(tap, tap)*, It's

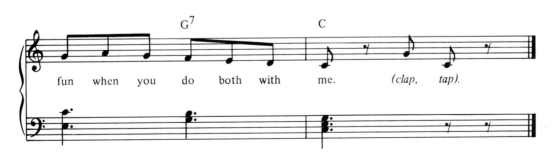

fun when you do both with me. *(clap, tap)*.

STEPHEN

M.K.B.

Mary Kay Bottens

Ste-phen was a man   Full of faith and power.

Ste-phen loved the Lord   Ev - en in his dark-est hour.

Ste-phen preached to men,   But their hearts were full of sin.   And they

stoned him,   They stoned this man of God.

PAUL AND SILAS

(Tune: "Here We Go 'Round the Mulberry Bush")

Paul and Silas prayed and sang,
Prayed and sang, prayed and sang.
Paul and Silas prayed and sang,
Oh, praise the name of Jesus!

Paul was safe in a fearful storm,
Fearful storm, fearful storm.
Paul was safe in a fearful storm,
Oh, praise the name of Jesus!

JESUS IN THE TEMPLE

Based on
Luke 2:46-49

John Leinbaugh

I WAS BLIND BUT NOW I SEE

N.L.S.

Norman L. Starks

"I was blind but now I see; Thank You, Lord, for heal-ing me!" Said the blind man Je - sus healed near Jer - i - cho._____ "What a hap - py, hap - py day, When King Je - sus came my way; Now I'll fol - low Him wher - ev - er He will go!"_____

NOAH

D.I.B.   Doris I. Black

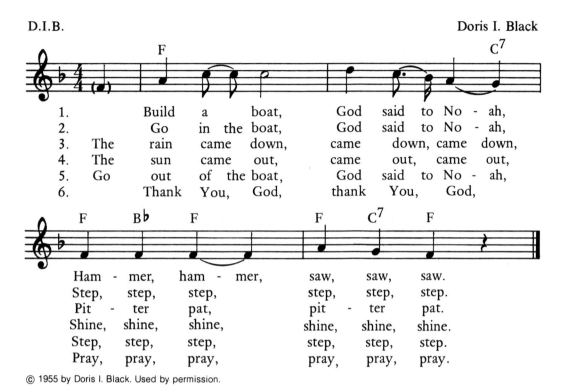

1. Build a boat, God said to No - ah,
2. Go in the boat, God said to No - ah,
3. The rain came down, came down, came down,
4. The sun came out, came out, came out,
5. Go out of the boat, God said to No - ah,
6. Thank You, God, thank You, God,

Ham - mer, ham - mer, saw, saw, saw.
Step, step, step, step, step, step.
Pit - ter pat, pit - ter pat.
Shine, shine, shine, shine, shine, shine.
Step, step, step, step, step, step.
Pray, pray, pray, pray, pray, pray.

COME UNTO ME

D.I.B.   Doris I. Black

The dis - ci - ples said, "No! You must go. Je - sus you can - not see." The

chil - dren were sad, Je - sus made them glad when He said "Come un - to me."

TEN LEPERS

R. B.

Ramona Brown

1. Hold up appropriate fingers. 2. Clap in rhythm. 3. Can hold up fingers and clap in rhythm or just hold up fingers or clap only.

© 1975 by Ramona Brown. Used by permission.

MARCHING AROUND JERICHO

M.H.F.

Marie H. Frost

God said, "March, march, march a - round Jer - i - cho.

Left, right, left, right, round and a - round you shall go."

One time, two times, three, four, five_ and six, And the

sev - enth time they marched a - round down came the bricks!

From *Songs for Preschoolers*, © 1977 by Marie H. Frost. Used by permission.

ABRAHAM AND SARAH

(Tune: "Did You Ever See a Lassie?")

Abraham and Sarah
Both wanted a baby.
God sent baby Isaac
To be their sweet boy.

—*Lynn Pratt*

BABY MOSES

Thea Cannon   Nancy Taylor

1. *Form basket with arms.* 2. *Rock "basket" back and forth.* 3. *Move arm outward.* 4. *Lift head and look up.*
5. *Run hands down sides to indicate elegant dress.*

DANIEL PRAYED

(Tune: "Mary Had a Little Lamb")

Daniel prayed to God each day,
God each day, God each day;
Daniel prayed to God each day;
He always prayed each day.

I will pray to God each day,
God each day, God each day;
I will pray to God each day;
I'll always pray each day.

BRAVE DANIEL IN THE LIONS' DEN

D.W.

Don Whitman

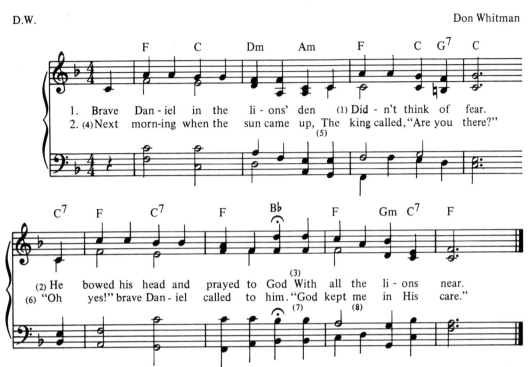

1. Brave Dan - iel in the li - ons' den (1) Did - n't think of fear.
2. (4) Next morn-ing when the sun came up, The king called, "Are you there?"
(5)

(2) He bowed his head and prayed to God With all the li - ons near. (3)
(6) "Oh yes!" brave Dan - iel called to him. "God kept me in His care." (7) (8)

1. Shake head. 2. Bow head and fold hands. 3. Hands outspread. 4. Make sun with hands. 5. Left hand cupped to mouth.
6. Right hand cupped to mouth. 7. Point upward. 8. Point to self.

ELIJAH

D. I. B.

Doris I. Black

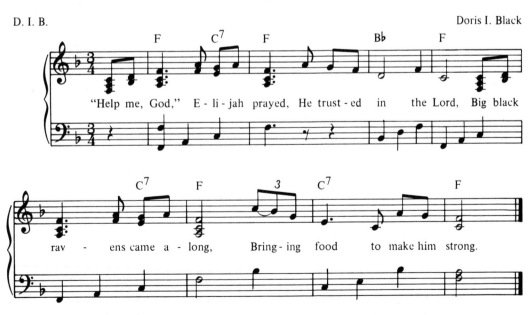

"Help me, God," E - li - jah prayed, He trust - ed in the Lord, Big black

rav - ens came a - long, Bring-ing food to make him strong.

JESUS! HE MADE THE BLIND MAN SEE

M. K. B.

Mary Kay Bottens

Je - sus! He made the blind man see!

Je - sus! He made the blind man see! Took some dirt, made some clay,*

Said, "Go, wash in the pool to-day!" Je - sus! He made the blind man see!

* *These words may be spoken if desired.*

GOD MADE EVERYTHING

D.I.B.

Doris I. Black

1. God made ev-'ry-thing big and small, ti-ny and tall,
2. God made rain to fall, rain to fall, rain to fall,
3. God made sun to shine, sun to shine, sun to shine,
4. God made birds to sing, tweet, tweet, tweet, tweet, tweet, tweet,

God made ev - 'ry-thing, yes, He made them all.
God made rain to fall, yes, He made it fall.
God made sun to shine, yes, He made it shine.
God made birds to sing, yes, He made them sing.

JONAH

P. H.

Patricia Hetrick

1. Jo - nah said, "I (1) will not go! The
2. (6) Jo - nah prayed in - side the fish — as

Lord will not find me; I will (2) flee up - on the sea." But God pre - pared a
sor - ry as could be; in the (7) mid - dle of the sea. God's great fish put him
(3)

(3) great big fish To__ teach him he must go—be - cause the Lord said so. (5)
on that shore; Jo - nah learned what he must say—o - beyed· the Lord that day.
(4)

Actions: 1. Shake head. 2. Running motions with fingers. 3. Make huge circles with arms. 4. Shake index finger.
5. Point up. 6. Fold hands as in prayer. 7. Hands out, palms up.

THE GOOD SAMARITAN

M.K.B.

Mary Kay Bottens

1. One day a man was walk-ing down to Jer - i - cho, When sud - den - ly some thieves rushed down up - on the road. They stripped him of his rai - ment and they wound - ed him. Then hur - ried off to car - ry on their lives of sin.
2. By chance there came a cer - tain priest a - long that way, But he just passed the man with - out a word to say, And like - wise came a Le - vite who was filled with pride, And he, too, hur - ried o - ver to the oth - er side.
3. When who but a Sa - mar - i - tan should come a - long, He had com - pas - sion on him; he knew right from wrong. He bound his wounds and lift - ed him up - on his beast; He paid for lodg - ing for him 'til his pain had ceased.
4. And so this is the ques - tion, which one of these three Was then the kind of neigh - bor you and I should be? Of course, the an - swer's clear — the good Sa - mar - i - tan. So fol - low his ex - am - ple — it's the Mas - ter's plan.

THAT YE MIGHT BELIEVE

John 20:31
P.H.

Patricia Hetrick

TRUST IN THE LORD

Psalm 37:3
(Tune: "Here We Go 'Round the Mulberry Bush")

Trust in the Lord, and always do good.
Trust in the Lord, and always do good.
Trust in the Lord, and always do good.
The Bible tells us to.

—*Sandra Maddux*

PLEASING GOD

Jean Baxendale

Linda Broyles

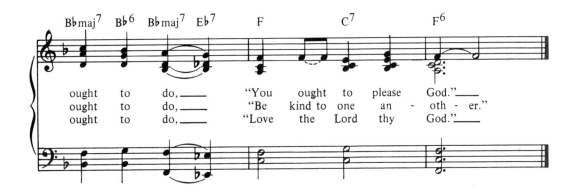

ought to do, _____ "You ought to please God." _____
ought to do, _____ "Be kind to one an - oth - er."
ought to do, _____ "Love the Lord thy God." _____

I WILL TRUST

S. E.

Sarah Eberle

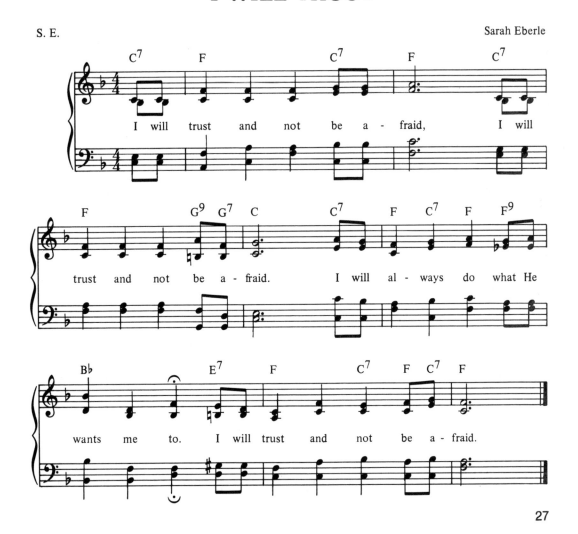

I will trust and not be a - fraid, I will

trust and not be a - fraid. I will al - ways do what He

wants me to. I will trust and not be a - fraid.

A GOOD THING

Psalm 92:1

S.E.

Sarah Eberle

It is a good thing to give thanks to the Lord; it is a good thing, a good thing. It is a good thing to give thanks to the Lord; it is a good, good thing.

PRAISE YE THE LORD

Psalm 150: 1

S. E.

Sarah Eberle

Praise ye the Lord._____ Praise ye the Lord._____ Praise Him for His

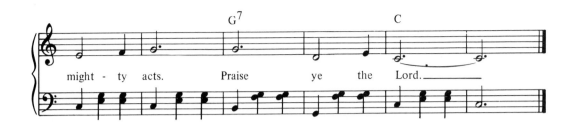

LET US LOVE ONE ANOTHER

I John 4:7 (N.A.S.V.)
M. H. F.

Marie H. Frost
Arr. by Mary McCann

THIS IS MY BELOVED SON

Matthew 17:5
M.K.B.

Mary Kay Bottens

LET THE LITTLE ONES COME UNTO ME

D. F. P.

Dorothy F. Poulton

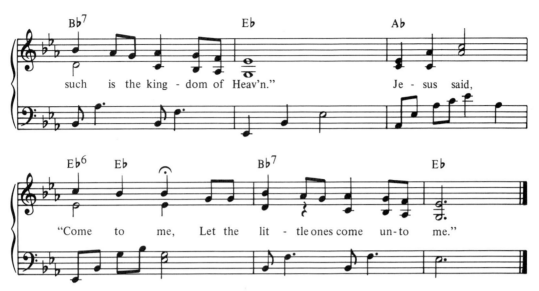

such is the king - dom of Heav'n." Je - sus said,
"Come to me, Let the lit - tle ones come un - to me."

FOLLOW HIM

S. E.

Sarah Eberle

If the Lord be God, fol - low Him.

If the Lord be God, fol - low Him. E - li - jah on the moun - tain

showed the Lord is God. If the Lord be God, fol - low Him.

LET EVERYTHING THAT HAS BREATH

Psalm 150:6

S.E.

Sarah Eberle

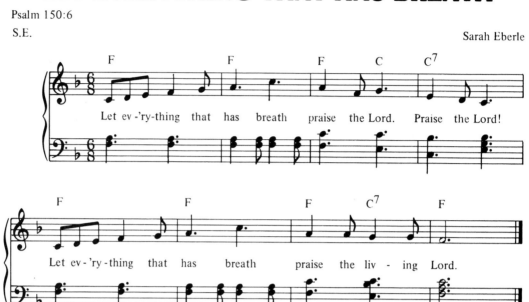

HE CARETH FOR YOU

E. P.

Eleanor Pankow

IN GOD'S HOUSE

D.E.

Dana Eynon
Arr. by Alice Koerner

1. God's house is a house of prayer, So soft-ly will I walk, And
2. In God's house I'll say a prayer, And praise to Him I'll sing, And

soft-ly will I talk. God's house is a house of prayer, And He is with me there.
gifts to Him I'll bring. In God's house I'll say a prayer For He is with me there.

INTO THE HOUSE OF THE LORD

M. A. S.

Mildred Adair Stagg

In - to the house of the Lord! In - to the house of the Lord!

"I was glad when they said un-to me, Let us go in-to the house of the Lord."

HERE IN OUR FATHER'S HOUSE

Mrs. C.B.P.

Mrs. C. B. Palmer

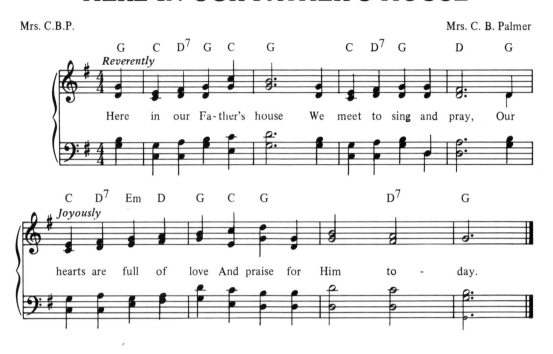

Here in our Fa-ther's house We meet to sing and pray, Our
hearts are full of love And praise for Him to - day.

THIS IS GOD'S HOUSE

Louise M. Oglevee

William G. Oglevee

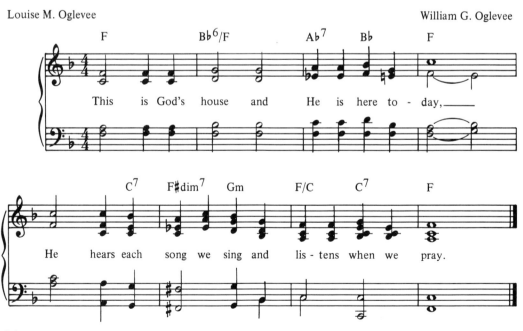

This is God's house and He is here to - day,____
He hears each song we sing and lis - tens when we pray.

HAPPY AT CHURCH

B.A.   Betty Aldridge

I like to go to church. I like to go to church. I'm
*hap-py, hap-py, hap-py. I like to go to church.

*Clap hands on "happy, happy, happy."

WE WILL GO TO CHURCH

S. T.   Sylvia Tester

Step, step, step, step, We will go to church.

WE'RE HERE IN OUR CHURCH

(Tune: "The More We Get Together.")

We are glad we are together,
   Together, together.
We are glad we are together,
We're here in our church.
Here are Cindy and Mary,*
And Robert, and David,
We are glad we are together,
We're here in our church.

                —Dot Cachiaras

*Use names of children in class.

I LOVE TO GO TO CHURCH

(Tune: "Farmer in the Dell")

I love to go to church;
I love to go to church.
With all the other boys and girls
   (or moms and dads),
I love to go to church.

                —Dot Cachiaras

GOD LOVES ME

P. J. W.

Phyllis J. Warfel

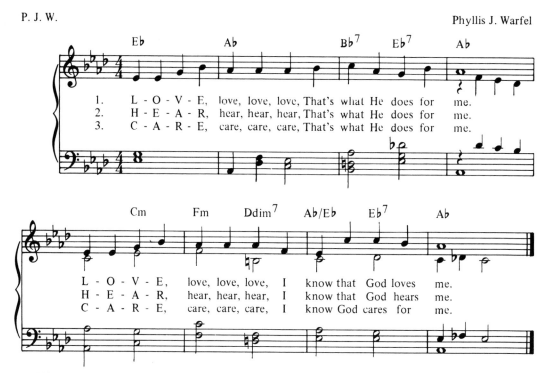

1. L - O - V - E, love, love, love, That's what He does for me.
2. H - E - A - R, hear, hear, hear, That's what He does for me.
3. C - A - R - E, care, care, care, That's what He does for me.

L - O - V - E, love, love, love, I know that God loves me.
H - E - A - R, hear, hear, hear, I know that God hears me.
C - A - R - E, care, care, care, I know God cares for me.

GOD IS EVER NEAR ME

M. A.

Mildred Adair

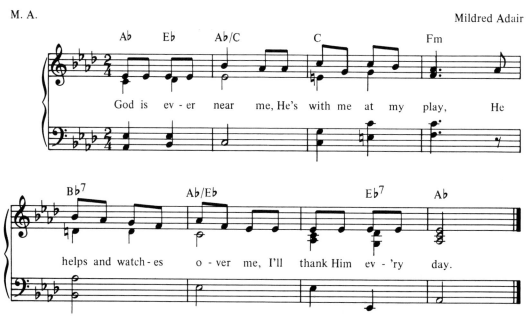

God is ev-er near me, He's with me at my play, He helps and watch-es o-ver me, I'll thank Him ev-'ry day.

THE LITTLE CHILDREN KNOW

M. A.

Mildred Adair

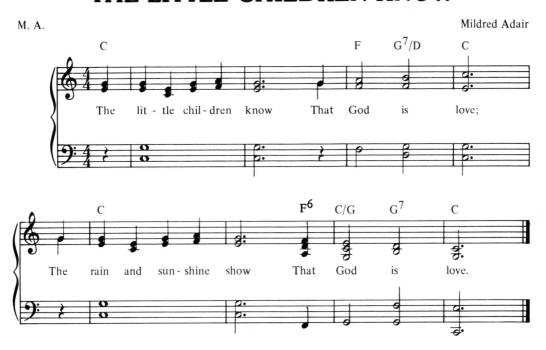

The lit-tle chil-dren know That God is love;

The rain and sun-shine show That God is love.

SING, LITTLE CHILDREN, SING

Mattie C. Leatherwood

Mildred Adair Stagg

Sing, lit-tle chil-dren, sing, sing, Sing lit-tle chil-dren, sing.

God is good, He cares for you, Sing, lit-tle chil-dren, sing.

THE LORD IS MY SHEPHERD

D. F. P.

Dorothy F. Poulton

1. "The Lord is my shep - herd," Was Da - vid's love - ly song:
2. "The Lord is my shep - herd," Sang Da - vid to his sheep:
3. "The Lord is my shep - herd," There's noth - ing then to fear;

"The Lord is my shep - herd," I'll sing it all day long.
"The Lord is my shep - herd," His watch o'er me He'll keep.
"The Lord is my shep - herd," I know He's al - ways near.

GOD IS GOOD

S. T.

Sylvia Tester

God is good. God is good. God is good.

GOD KEEPS HIS PROMISES

(Tune: Chorus of "Rescue the Perishing")

God keeps His promises;
He's always faithful;
God keeps His promises;
They will come true.

I WILL TRUST IN GOD

(Tune: "Fishers of Men")

I will trust and not be afraid;
Not be afraid;
Not be afraid;
I will trust and not be afraid;
I will trust in God.

AT WORK OR AT PLAY, GOD SEES

M. A.

Mildred Adair

1. At work or at play, God sees, God sees. By
2. When good and when true, God knows, God knows. His
3. A soft whis-pered prayer, God hears, God hears. A

night or by day, God sees, He sees.
will try to do, God knows, He knows.
song bright and fair, God hears, He hears.

PLEASE HIM, PLEASE HIM

(Tune: "Praise Him, Praise Him")

Please Him, please Him,
All you little children.
God loves you, God loves you.

Please Him, please Him,
All you little children.
God loves you, God loves you.

GOD CARES

D. F. R.

Dorothy Fay Richards

God sees, God knows, God hears, God cares.

39

THE BEST BOOK IN THE WORLD

Marie H. Frost

Marie H. Frost
Arr. by Mary McCann

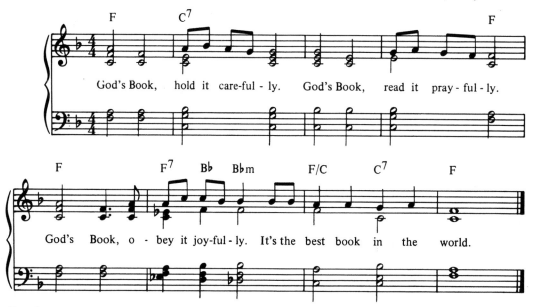

God's Book, hold it care-ful-ly. God's Book, read it pray-ful-ly.

God's Book, o-bey it joy-ful-ly. It's the best book in the world.

From *Songs for Preschoolers*, © 1977 by Marie H. Frost. Used by permission.

THANK YOU, GOD

J.L.

Joan Leach

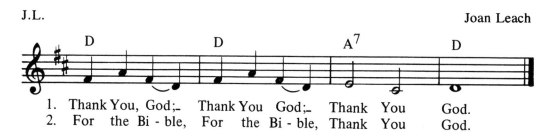

1. Thank You, God;— Thank You God;— Thank You God.
2. For the Bi-ble, For the Bi-ble, Thank You God.

THE BIBLE

S.T.

Sylvia Tester

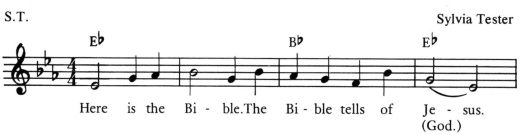

Here is the Bi-ble. The Bi-ble tells of Je-sus. (God.)

40

Here is the Bi - ble. The Bi - ble tells of Je - sus. (God.)

BIBLE SONG

Betty Aldridge

B.A.

I o-pen my Bi - ble and read. ___ My Bi - ble tells a-bout

Je - sus. I o - pen my Bi - ble and read. ___

IN HIS BIBLE BOOK

Lydia Adams

Janet Gallup

What does my Je - sus teach me in His Bi - ble

book? He teach - es me to love* Him in His Bi - ble book.

*help, praise, trust

MY BIBLE TELLS A STORY

I.H.

Imogene Humphrey

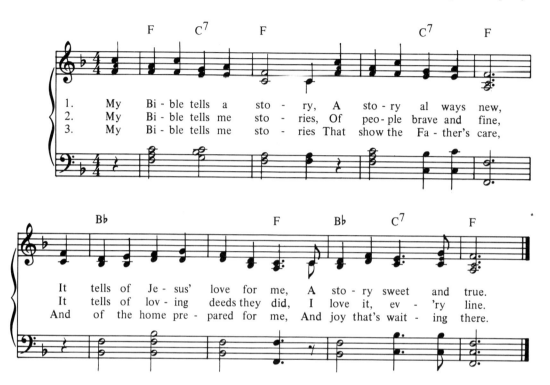

1. My Bi - ble tells a sto - ry, A sto - ry al ways new,
2. My Bi - ble tells me sto - ries, Of peo - ple brave and fine,
3. My Bi - ble tells me sto - ries That show the Fa - ther's care,

It tells of Je - sus' love for me, A sto - ry sweet and true.
It tells of lov - ing deeds they did, I love it, ev - 'ry line.
And of the home pre - pared for me, And joy that's wait - ing there.

GOD'S BOOK TELLS ME

Aurora M. Shumate

Clara Lee Parker

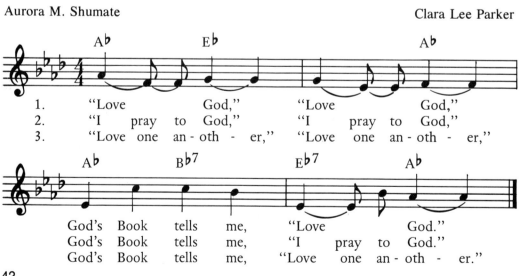

1. "Love God," "Love God,"
2. "I pray to God," "I pray to God,"
3. "Love one an - oth - er," "Love one an - oth - er,"

God's Book tells me, "Love God."
God's Book tells me, "I pray to God."
God's Book tells me, "Love one an - oth - er."

BELIEVE, OBEY, AND SHARE IT

Wanda Hayes

Janet Gallup

1. I love the Bi - ble sto - ries My tea - cher tells to me. I
2. The Bi - ble tells of Je - sus, God's Son, so kind and good. I
3. I like to tell the sto - ry Of Je - sus, God's own Son. And

know that they can help me Learn how a child should be.
will o - bey His les - sons, And do the things I should.
I will glad - ly share it; It is for ev - 'ry - one!

Be - lieve, o - bey, and share it. The Book from God is true. Be -

lieve, o - bey, and share it. This I will glad - ly do.

IT'S A HAPPY DAY

B. L. H.

Barbara Le Hays

1. Sang the lit - tle bird on the lit - tle tree, "In a ver - y spe - cial
2. Sang the lit - tle cat climb - ing on the fence, "In a ver - y spe - cial
3. Sang the lit - tle dog run - ning on the road, "In a ver - y spe - cial
4. So we all should sing this___ hap - py song, "In a ver - y spe - cial

way, The world is God's and I am God's, It's a
way, The world is God's and I am God's, It's a
way, The world is God's and I am God's, It's a
way, The world is God's and we are God's, It's a

tweet, tweet hap - py day;___ It's a tweet, tweet hap - py day!"
me - ow hap - py day;___ It's a me - ow hap - py day!"
woof! woof! hap - py day;___ It's a woof! woof! hap - py day!"
hap - hap hap - py day;___ It's a hap - hap hap - py day!"

Encourage the children to add verses of their own.

© 1967 by Barbara LeHays. Used by permission.

44

THE GROWING SONG

Diane McIntyre

Joy Grewell

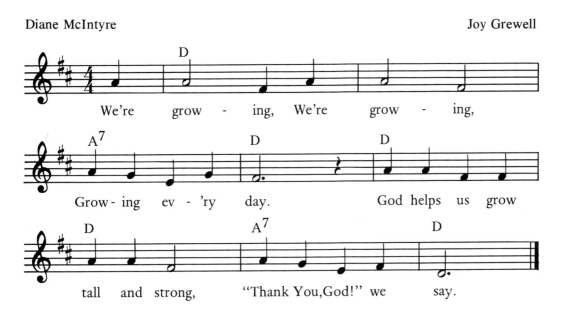

We're grow - ing, We're grow - ing,

Grow - ing ev - 'ry day. God helps us grow

tall and strong, "Thank You, God!" we say.

OH, WHO MAKES THE FLOWERS?

M. A.

Mildred Adair

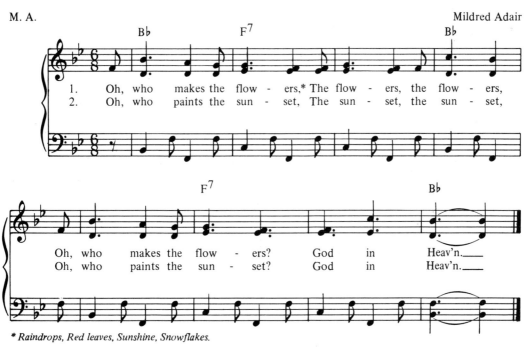

1. Oh, who makes the flow - ers,* The flow - ers, the flow - ers,
2. Oh, who paints the sun - set, The sun - set, the sun - set,

Oh, who makes the flow - ers? God in Heav'n.
Oh, who paints the sun - set? God in Heav'n.

Raindrops, Red leaves, Sunshine, Snowflakes.

45

DID YOU LISTEN TO THE WIND?

M.A.   Mildred Adair

Did you lis-ten to the wind as it blew to-day,

"Oo - oo - oo"? Did you lis-ten to the wind and—

hear it say, "God loves you"?

GOD MADE THE DOGGIES

S.T.   Sylvia Tester

God made the dog-gies that go bark! bark! bark!
        kit-ties   meow! meow! meow!
        etc.

God made the dog-gies that go bark! bark! bark!
        kit-ties   meow! meow! meow!

GOD'S WORLD

J.M.G.

Joy M. Grewell

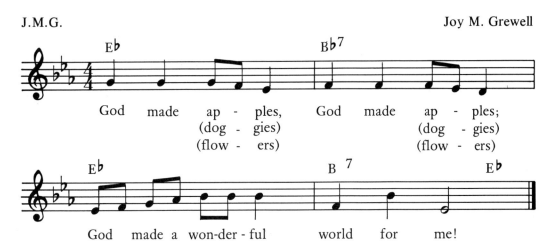

God made ap - ples, God made ap - ples;
(dog - gies) (dog - gies)
(flow - ers) (flow - ers)

God made a won-der-ful world for me!

GOD MADE

B.A.

Betty Aldridge

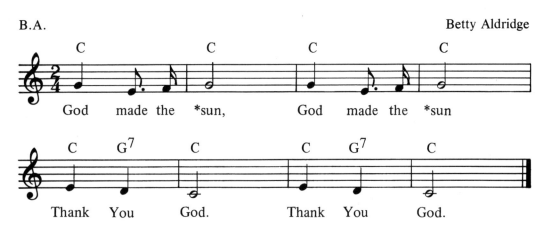

God made the *sun, God made the *sun

Thank You God. Thank You God.

*moon, flow'r, bird, dog, cat, etc.

I'M SPECIAL

B.A.

Betty Aldridge

I'm spe-cial, I'm spe-cial. God made me!

(Substitute toddler's name for "I'm" and "me.")

THE RAINDROPS FALL

M. A.

Mildred Adair

The rain-drops fall with a pit-ter, pat-ter, pit,*

Pit-ter, pat-ter, pit, pit-ter, pat-ter, pit, The

rain-drops fall with a pit-ter, pat-ter, pit, Show-ing God's great love.

*Pat hands together to indicate "soft" rain or "hard" rain.

GOD MADE FOOD

B.A.

Betty Aldridge

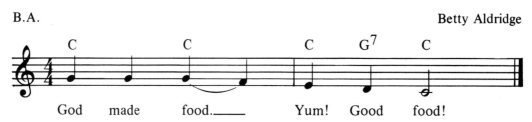

God made food.___ Yum! Good food!

(Repeat, substituting specific foods for the word "food.")

GOD MADE MY FAMILY

J. M. G.   Joy M. Grewell

F   Bb⁶   Bb

1. God__ made my Mom-my, and God__ made__ me,
2. Thank You, God, for Mom-my,____ and for mak-ing me,

C⁷   F

God__ made my Dad-dy, and my whole fam - i - ly!
Thank You, God, for Dad-dy, and my whole fam - i - ly!

ALL THINGS WERE MADE BY HIM

John 1:3
M. A.   Mildred Adair

D   A⁷   D   Bm   E⁷   A⁷

All things were made by Him,   All things were made by Him,

D   G   D/A   A⁷   D

God's great love   and God's great pow'r, All things were made by Him.

J-E-S-U-S

P. H.

Patricia Hetrick

J - E - S - U - S — Spells a friend that you should know.

J - E - S - U - S — Spells the One who loves me so.

J - E - S - U - S — Spells the One that I love best!

And His Word I will o - bey._____

JESUS NEVER FAILS

(Tune: "Row, Row, Row Your Boat")

Jesus never fails,
Never, never fails.
I'm glad, so glad
Jesus never fails.

HE'S SPEAKING

D. C.

Dot Cachiaras
Arr. by Cynthia Winter

Je - sus Christ is God's own Son and He loves us ev - 'ry - one.___ He clear - ly speaks to us to - day thru the Bi - ble, lest we stray.___ He's

REFRAIN

speak - ing, He's speak - ing. Thru the Bi - ble He's speak - ing. He's speak - ing, He's speak - ing. If we love Him, we'll o - bey.

COME TO ME

S.T.

Sylvia Tester

"Come to me!" Je - sus said. "Hap - py chil - dren, come to me!"

I LOVE TO TELL ABOUT JESUS

D.W.

Don Whitman

I WILL FOLLOW JESUS

L.K.

LaVern Karns

1. Walk in place. 2. Clap hands. 3. Fold hands. 4. Point upward.

HALLELU

Sarah Eberle

Marian Bennett

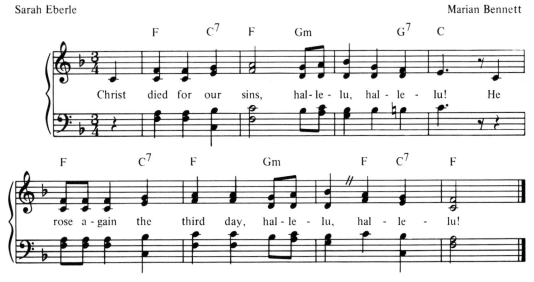

COME UNTO ME

L.K.

LaVern Karns

"Let the lit - tle chil - dren come un - to me.
Come un-to me. Come un-to me. Let the lit - tle chil - dren
come un-to me." Je - sus loves the chil - dren.

CLAP, CLAP YOUR HANDS FOR JOY

M. A.

Mildred Adair

Clap, clap your hands for joy, Clap, clap your hands for love, I

know that Je - sus Christ is good, And that He lives a - bove.

JESUS' LITTLE LAMB

L.K.

LaVern Karns

1. I am Je - sus' lit - tle lamb.
2. I am His and He is mine.

Hap - py all day long I am. He will keep me
I'm so hap - py all the time. Je - sus loves me!

safe I know. For I'm His lit - tle lamb.
This I know, For I'm His lit - tle lamb.

BELIEVE IT!

S.E.

Sarah Eberle

JESUS IS THE SON OF GOD

C.D.W.

Cynthia D. Wagner

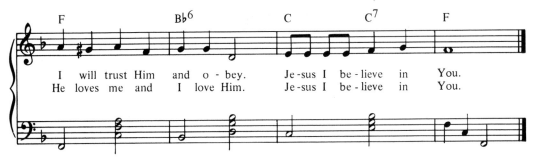

I will trust Him and o - bey. Je-sus I be - lieve in You.
He loves me and I love Him. Je-sus I be - lieve in You.

THE TWELVE APOSTLES

(Tune: "Ten Little Indians")

One-two-three-four-five apostles
Six-seven-eight-nine-ten apostles
Eleven and twelve apostles
Working for the Lord.

You and I can work for Jesus.
You and I can work for Jesus.
You and I can work for Jesus.
We are helpers, too.

OUR BEST FRIEND IS JESUS

Carolyn Dobbs
Alice Koerner

Roger and Alice Koerner

1. Our best friend is Je - sus; He's with us ev - 'ry day,
2. Je - sus al - ways loves us, And tells us what to do.

When we're sad or hap - py, At home, at school, at play.
We can make Him hap - py, If we will love Him, too.

MY BEST FRIEND IS JESUS

M.A.S.

Mildred Adair Stagg

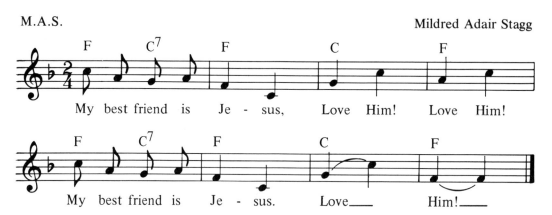

My best friend is Je-sus, Love Him! Love Him!

My best friend is Je-sus. Love____ Him!____

JESUS

(Tune: "Here We Go 'Round the Mulberry Bush")

Oh, Jesus is the Son of God,
Son of God, Son of God.
Oh, Jesus is the Son of God,
He healed the crippled man.*

*He made the blind man see.
He made the dead girl live.

I WILL LIVE FOR HIM

(Tune: "Mary Had a Little Lamb")

Jesus is the Son of God,
Son of God, Son of God.
Jesus is the Son of God,
I will live for Him.*
—Carmen C. Fellows

*And He cares for me.

I LOVE JESUS

S.T.

Sylvia Tester

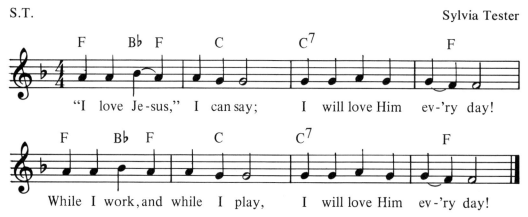

"I love Je-sus," I can say; I will love Him ev-'ry day!

While I work, and while I play, I will love Him ev-'ry day!

JESUS, THE SON OF GOD

D.W.

Don Whitman

1. Je - sus, the Son of God   Came from Heav'n a - bove;
2. Je - sus, the Son of God,   Lord of life was He;
3. Je - sus, the Son of God   Died up - on the cross.
4. Je - sus, the Son of God,   We will fol - low Thee.

Sent to us from God on high To show us His great love.
Healed the blind and raised the dead, That we His pow'r might see.
Lives a - gain to give us life If we will in Him trust.
Tell us what to do and say And help us true to be.

JESUS IS GOD'S SON

B.E.

Barbara Ebert
Arranged by Morine Barnes

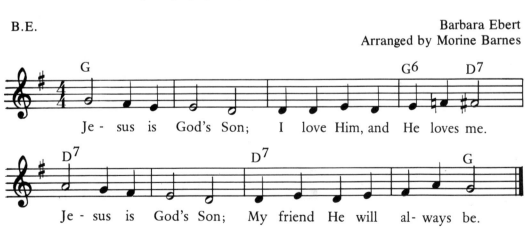

Je - sus is God's Son;   I love Him, and He loves me.

Je - sus is God's Son;   My friend He will al - ways be.

JESUS, GOD'S GIFT

B.W.

Becky Wade

Je-sus is God's gift of love. Je-sus came down from a-bove.
Je-sus loves you and loves me. Je-sus, our best friend is He.

I LOVE JESUS BEST OF ALL

J. G.

Janet Gallup

I love Je-sus best of all — I love Je-sus best of all.
I love Je-sus best of all. I know that He loves me.

SMILE, MARY, SMILE

B.E.

Barbara Ebert
Arranged by Morine Barnes

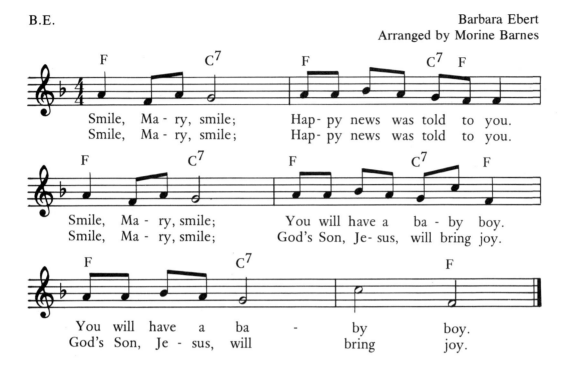

THE SHEPHERDS WALKED ON TIPTOE

B.E.

Barbara Ebert
Arranged by Morine Barnes

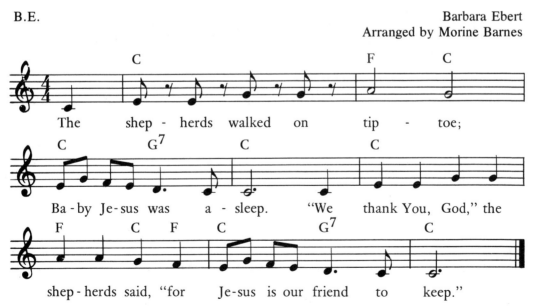

JESUS WAS BORN

S.T.   Sylvia Tester

Je - sus was born one hap - py day.

Je - sus was born one hap - py day.

JESUS GREW AND GREW

B.E.   Barbara Ebert
                                                       Arranged by Morine Barnes

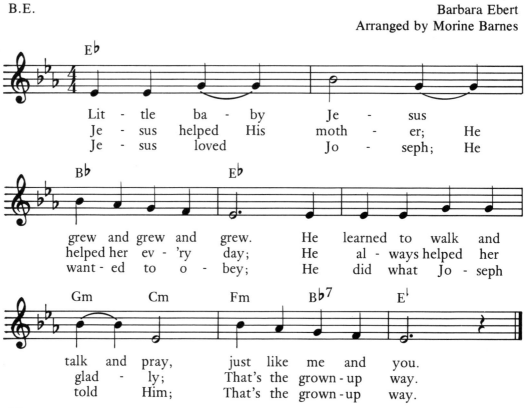

Lit - tle ba - by Je - sus
Je - sus helped His moth - er; He
Je - sus loved Jo - seph; He

grew and grew and grew. He learned to walk and
helped her ev - 'ry day; He al - ways helped her
want - ed to o - bey; He did what Jo - seph

talk and pray, just like me and you.
glad - ly; That's the grown - up way.
told Him; That's the grown - up way.

62

RING, BELLS, RING!

J.C.

Judy Cook

Hear the birds sing, let the bells ring. It's Christ-mas morn.
Sing a glad song, all the day long. Je-sus is born.

Let us join our hands and sing praise to Je-sus Christ, our

King. Ring! Ring! Bells, ring!

ROCK BABY JESUS

B.A.

Betty Aldridge

Rock ba-by Je-sus, Rock Him, rock Him,

Rock ba-by Je-sus, Rock Him now.___

63

CHRISTMAS BELLS ARE RINGING

M.H.F.

Marie H. Frost

1. Ring - a - ling - a, Ring - a - ling - a, Christ-mas bells are
2. Ring - a - ling - a, Ring - a - ling - a, What do Christ-mas

ring - ing, Sing - a - ling - a, Sing - a - ling - a,
bells say? Ba - by Je - sus In a man-ger was

1. Hap - py chil - dren sing - ing.
2. born on Christ-mas day.

From *Songs for Preschoolers*, © 1977 by Marie H. Frost. Used by permission.

LET US BE HAPPY

J.C.

Judy Cook

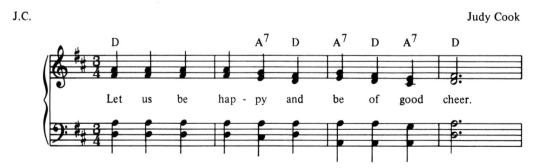

Let us be hap - py and be of good cheer.

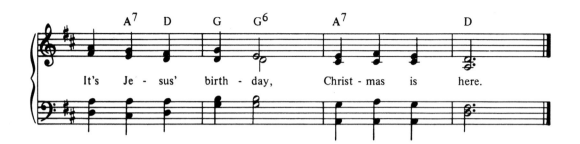

It's Je - sus' birth - day, Christ - mas is here.

GOOD CHEER

J.C.

Judy Cook

Good cheer, good cheer. Let us be joy - ful!

Good cheer, good cheer. Join hands and sing.

Good cheer, good cheer. It's Je - sus' birth - day.

Good cheer, good cheer. Let the bells ring! *Good cheer! (ring bells)*

HERE WE COME TO BETHLEHEM

E.F.B.

Emma F. Bush

1. Here we come to Beth - le - hem, Here we come to Beth - le - hem,
2. Here we see the shep-herds kneel, Here we see the shep-herds kneel,
3. Here the Wise-men bring their gifts, Here the Wise-men bring their gifts,
4. We will sing on Christ-mas day, We will sing on Christ-mas day,

Here we come to Beth - le - hem, To see the ba - by Je - sus.
Here we see the shep-herds kneel, Be - fore the ba - by Je - sus.
Here the Wise-men bring their gifts, To give the ba - by Je - sus.
We will sing on Christ-mas day, Praise to the ba - by Je - sus.

SEE THE STAR

A. K.

Alice Koerner

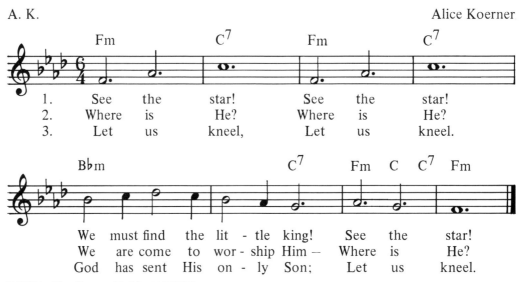

1. See the star! See the star!
2. Where is He? Where is He?
3. Let us kneel, Let us kneel.

We must find the lit - tle king! See the star!
We are come to wor - ship Him — Where is He?
God has sent His on - ly Son; Let us kneel.

OUR OFFERING SONG

J. G.

Janet Gallup

We're hap - py, so hap - py! Bring-ing our of-fering to Je - sus. We're

hap - py, so hap - py! Bring-ing our of - fering to Him.___

Repeat as needed

I'M GIVING

A. K.

Alice Koerner

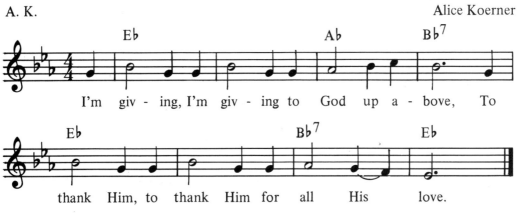

I'm giv - ing, I'm giv - ing to God up a - bove, To

thank Him, to thank Him for all His love.

IT IS MORE BLESSED

Acts 20:35

S.E.

Sarah Eberle

It is more bless - ed to give than to re - ceive. It is more bless - ed to give than to re - ceive. It is more bless - ed to give than to re - ceive. It is more bless - ed, It is more bless - ed. It is more bless - ed to give than to re - ceive.

GIVE UNTO THE LORD

L. K.

LaVern Karns

1. Give un-to the Lord with a cheer-ful heart, Give as He has giv-en un-to thee._____ Give un-to the Lord with a cheer-ful heart; This is what my Sav-ior teach-es me._____

2. Go in-to the world with the gos-pel news, Go and I will ev-er be with thee._____ Go in-to the world with the gos-pel news; This is what my Sav-ior teach-es me._____

FOR OUR CHURCH

L. Y.

Lorraine Yohe

Bless our off-'ring, dear__ God. It is for our church!

LOVING AND FORGIVING

P. J. W.

Phyllis J. Warfel

MOMMY LOVES ME

B.A.

Betty Aldridge

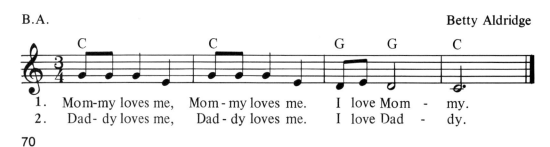

LET US LOVE ONE ANOTHER

N.L.S.

Norman L. Starks

Let us love one an-oth-er, Love one an-oth-er, Grow-ing and car-ing more each day. ___ O let us love one an-oth-er, Love one an-oth-er, Learn-ing to walk in Je-sus' way.

HELP ME TO FORGIVE

(Tune: "Row, Row, Row Your Boat")

Jesus, help me forgive,
Help me always forgive.
Even when I'm sad and hurt,
Help me to forgive.
—Wanda Pelfrey

VACATION TIME

Dorothy Fay Richards

Alice Koerner

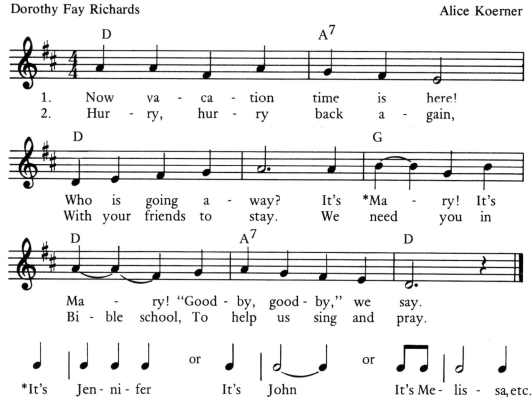

1. Now va - ca - tion time is here!
2. Hur - ry, hur - ry back a - gain,

Who is going a - way? It's *Ma - ry! It's
With your friends to stay. We need you in

Ma - ry! "Good - by, good - by," we say.
Bi - ble school, To help us sing and pray.

*It's Jen - ni - fer   It's John   It's Me - lis - sa, etc.

THANK-YOU SONG

J.B.

Jean Baxendale

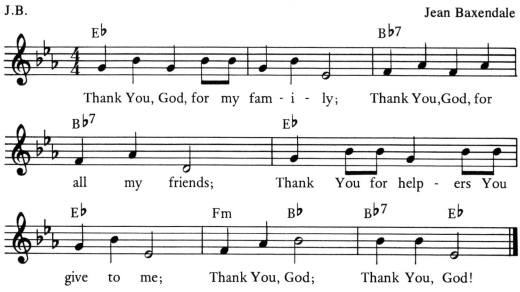

Thank You, God, for my fam - i - ly; Thank You, God, for

all my friends; Thank You for help - ers You

give to me; Thank You, God; Thank You, God!

IT'S DONE FOR CHRIST

P. H.

Patricia Hetrick

1. Sew, sew, sew with Dor-cas, a
2. Live, live, live like Dor-cas, and

coat or a dress for a poor child or moth-er.
do deeds of kind-ness in some way or oth-er.

In each seam goes love and serv-ice. It's
Share your bless-ings. Show your love._____ It's

Done for Christ when it's done for an-oth-er.

Actions for verse 1: 1. Pronounced up and down sewing motion. 2. Hands touch shoulder. 3. Hands hold out a gift.
4. With hand, measure child's height from floor. 5. Hand measures taller height. 6. Point up. 7. Reach out hands.

LET US PRAISE
GOD TOGETHER

Words adapted by
Sandra Maddux

Arranged from
"Let Us Break Bread Together"

Let us praise God to-geth-er to - day,____

____ Let us praise God to-geth-er to - day.____

____ As we come here to wor -ship Thank ing Him for

Je-sus Let us praise God to-geth-er to - day.____

SONG OF PRAISE

A.H.

Ann Hughes

1. Praise be to God! Praise be to God!
2. Je - sus, my friend, Je - sus, my friend,

Praise be to God for the gift of His Son!
He is be - side me where - ev - er I go.

Ba - by Je - sus we wor - ship to - day,
Je - sus, Je - sus is with me to - day,

Born in a man - ger and laid on the hay:
Guid - ing me, keep - ing me, lead - ing the way.

RHYTHM BAND PRAISE SONG

S.E.

Sarah Eberle

Praise God with the sticks. Praise God with the bells and tri-an-gle. Praise God with the drum and tam-bou-rine. Praise the King of Kings.

WAYS TO PRAISE GOD

S.E.

Sarah Eberle

Praise God by clap-ping your hands. Praise Him by sing-ing a song. Praise God by

76

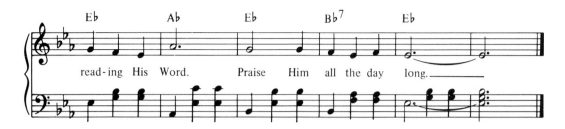

read-ing His Word. Praise Him all the day long._____

PRAISE GOD!

S.E.

Sarah Eberle

Praise God with a shout: The Lord, He is God!
(Shout)

Praise Him with a clap: clap - clap - clap - clap. Praise God with a song: The

Lord, He is God. Praise Him ev - 'ry way that you can.

ONE LITTLE VOICE

M.C.T.

Mabel C. Todd

One lit-tle voice to praise the Lord, Two lit-tle voi-ces to sing His Word,

All our lit-tle voi-ces with one ac-cord, We'll praise the Lord, praise the Lord.

DO NOT WORSHIP OTHER GODS

(Tune: "Mary Had a Little Lamb")

Do not worship other gods,
Other gods, other gods;
Do not worship other gods,
They're only made by hands!

We will worship God today,
God today, God today;
We will worship God today;
It is to Him we'll pray.

LET HIM SING PRAISES

(Tune: "Are You Sleeping?")

Is anyone cheerful? *(repeat)*
Let him sing. *(repeat)*
Let him sing praises *(repeat)*
To our King. *(repeat)*

—Judy Cook

WE THANK YOU, GOD IN HEAVEN

M.A.

Mildred Adair

We thank You, God in Heav - en, For Je - sus, for Je - sus.* We

thank You, God in Heav - en, For Je - sus.**

*For Mother; For Father, etc.   **For Mother dear; For Father dear, etc.
*Other people or things to be thankful for may be substituted.

LET'S BE VERY QUIET

D. F. R.

Dorothy Fay Richards

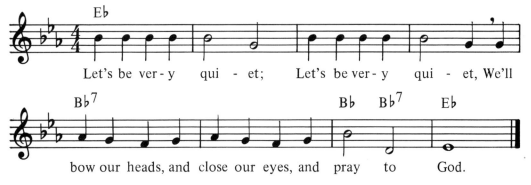

Let's be ver - y qui - et; Let's be ver - y qui - et, We'll

bow our heads, and close our eyes, and pray to God.

WHEN WE PRAY

Sandra Summers

Janet Gallup

We close our eyes and bow our heads, We
fold our hands to pray._____ We'll all be ver-y
qui - et now, And talk to God to - day._____

© 1965 by Janet Gallup. Used by permission.

I CAN TALK TO GOD

G.S.

Gertrude Shannon

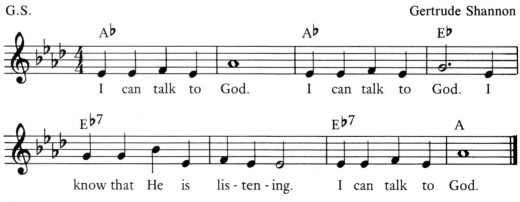

I can talk to God. I can talk to God. I
know that He is lis-ten-ing. I can talk to God.

80

NOW WE'LL TALK TO GOD

D.C.

Dot Cachiaras
Arr. by Michelle Pittinger

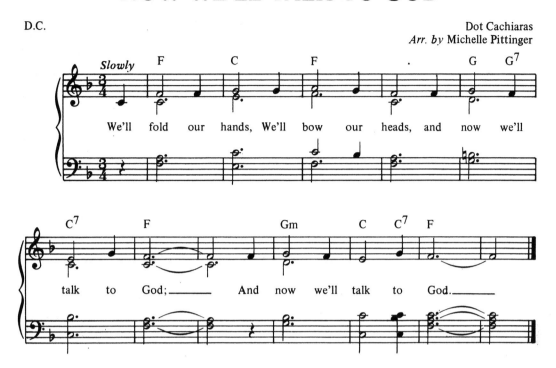

We'll fold our hands, We'll bow our heads, and now we'll talk to God;_____ And now we'll talk to God._____

GOD KNOWS MY NAME

S. M.

Sandra Maddux

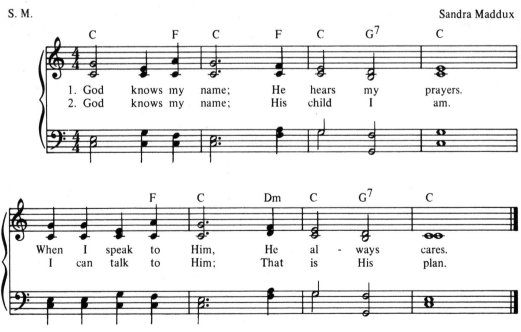

1. God knows my name; He hears my prayers.
2. God knows my name; His child I am.

When I speak to Him, He al - ways cares.
I can talk to Him; That is His plan.

WE THANK YOU, THANK YOU, GOD

S.T.

Sylvia Tester

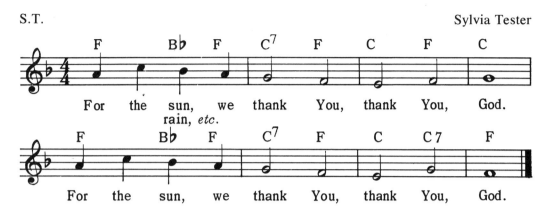

For the sun, we thank You, thank You, God.
rain, *etc.*

For the sun, we thank You, thank You, God.

I CAN PRAY TO GOD

D. F. R.

Dorothy Fay Richards

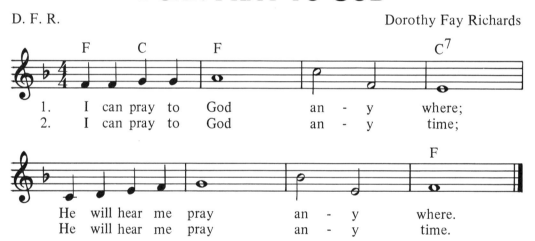

1. I can pray to God an - y where;
2. I can pray to God an - y time;

He will hear me pray an - y where.
He will hear me pray an - y time.

I THANK GOD

S. T.

Sylvia Tester

I thank God. I thank God. I thank God.

EV'RY DAY WE THANK YOU

M.A.

Mildred Adair

Ev -'ry day we thank You For bless-ings from a - bove;

Ev -'ry day we thank You For Your care and love. A - men.

THANK-YOU PRAYER

J.L.H.

Jenna Lusby Houp

Thank You, Lord, For giv-ing us this day. Thank You, Lord, For be-ing our friend.

Thank You, Lord, For show-ing us the way, Through Je - sus, A - men.

PLEASE GOD

Autoharp
or Guitar

Dale L. Aldridge

1. Will you share and be glad? Will you love and not feel bad?
2. I will share and be glad! I will love and not feel bad!

Will you try in man-y ways To please God?
I will try in man-y ways To please God!

The question and answer verses can be used in various ways.
1. The leader can sing the questions and the children respond with the second verse.
2. The children can sing the verses to each other.
3. The children can sing the questions to the teachers and the teachers respond with the answers.

A good way to end this activity would be to sing a final verse substituting "we" for the "I" of the second verse.

GOD WANTS ME TO DO RIGHT

D.C.

Dot Cachiaras
Arranged by Michelle Pittinger

1. God wants me to do right, do right, do right, God
2. God helps me to do right, do right, do right, God

TWO HELPING HANDS HAVE I

M. A.

Mildred Adair

GOD'S FRIENDS

C.C.F.

Carmen C. Fellows
Arranged by Michelle Pittinger

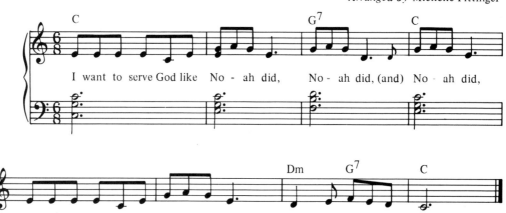

I want to serve God like No-ah did, No-ah did, (and) No-ah did,

I want to help God in my spe-cial way just like No-ah did.

LOVE ONE ANOTHER

Mattie C. Leatherwood

Mildred Adair Stagg

Love_* one an-oth-er, Love_ one an-oth-er,

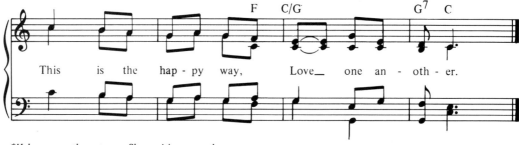

This is the hap-py way, Love_ one an-oth-er.

*Help one another, etc. – Share with one another, etc.

I WANT TO SPEAK FOR GOD

(Tune: "Mary Had a Little Lamb")

I want to speak for God,
Speak for God,
Speak for God.
I want to speak for God,
To please Him every day.

I want to sing for God,
Sing for God,
Sing for God.
I want to sing for God,
To please Him every day.

JESUS' HELPERS

A. K.

Alice Koerner

We are help-ing Je - sus when we help our friends on earth,

When we tell the sto - ry of Je - sus' hum - ble birth,

When we show to oth - ers kind and lov - ing care.

We are help - ing Je - sus when we go to Him in prayer.

SERVE THE LORD WITH GLADNESS

S.E.

Sarah Eberle

Serve the Lord with glad - ness: clap your hands!

Serve the Lord with glad - ness: clap your hands!

I CAN BE A HELPER

J.M.

Jean Maddux

1. Pe - ter* was a help - er, I can be one too.
2. I can set the ta - ble, That's what I can do.
3. I can pick my toys up, That's what I can do.

When I'm with my fam - 'ly, Just what can I do?
I can wash the dish - es, I can do that too.
I can fold the clothes, yes, I can do that too.

*Dorcas, or other Bible names

88

I'LL OBEY

Dot Cachiaras

D. C.

1. If my moth-er calls me When I'm hav-ing fun,
2. When my dad-dy calls to Help him in the yard,
3. When the traf-fic light blinks, This is what I know:
4. When my heav'n-ly Fa-ther Tells me to be kind

I will quit my play-ing, And to her I'll run.
I'll do all he asks me, For he works so hard.
Red means wait a mo-ment; Green means I can go.
In His book, the Bi-ble, I'll try hard to mind.

CHORUS

I'll o-bey! I'll o-bey! Quick-ly I'll o-bey!

A FRIEND OF GOD

Michelle Pittinger

M.P.

I want to be a friend of God; I want to be a friend of
God; so ev-'ry day I will be kind, I'll share my toys. I will o-bey.
(I will love Him, I'll speak for Him) I will o-bey.

89

A HELPER KIND AND GOOD

Mattie C. Leatherwood

Mildred Adair Stagg

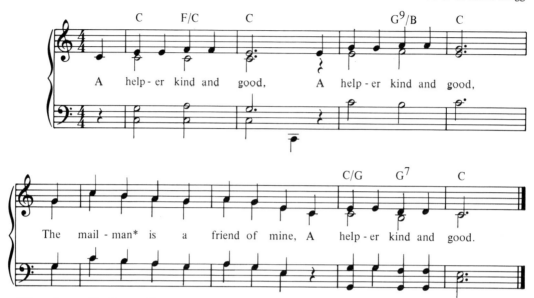

A help-er kind and good, A help-er kind and good,

The mail-man* is a friend of mine, A help-er kind and good.

*The policeman; The fireman; The grocer; The farmer; The doctor, etc.

I GIVE MYSELF TO JESUS

Catherine Lee

LaVern Karns

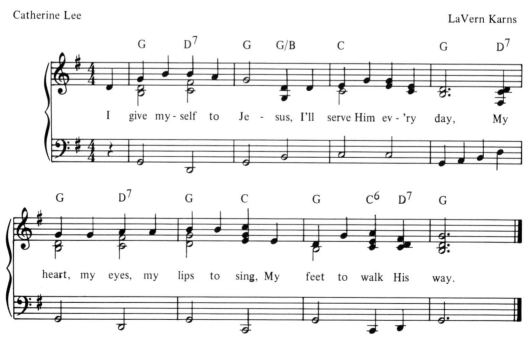

I give my-self to Je-sus, I'll serve Him ev-'ry day, My

heart, my eyes, my lips to sing, My feet to walk His way.

BRING YOUR CHAIRS

B.A.   Betty Aldridge

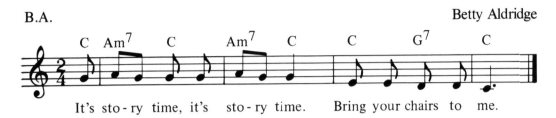

It's sto-ry time, it's sto-ry time.   Bring your chairs to me.

PLAYTIME'S DONE

B.A.   Betty Aldridge

*Play - time's   done, ____   play - time's   done.

Now   it's   time   for   sto - ry ____   fun!

*Yes, dear Brian, etc.

IT IS STORY TIME

B.A.   Betty Aldridge

Time to put the *toys on the shelf.   It is sto-ry   time.

*Substitute blocks, puzzles, etc.

IT'S BIBLE TIME

(Tune: "London Bridge")

Gather 'round, it's Bible time,
Bible time, Bible time;
Gather 'round, it's Bible time,
Come and listen.

IT'S TIME TO WORSHIP GOD

J. A.

Janet Ashford

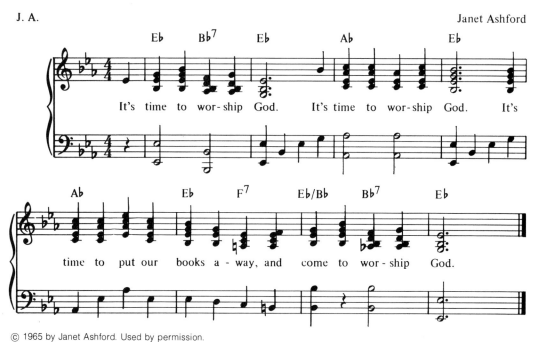

It's time to wor-ship God. It's time to wor-ship God. It's time to put our books a-way, and come to wor-ship God.

WE THANK YOU, LORD

J.A.

Janet Ashford

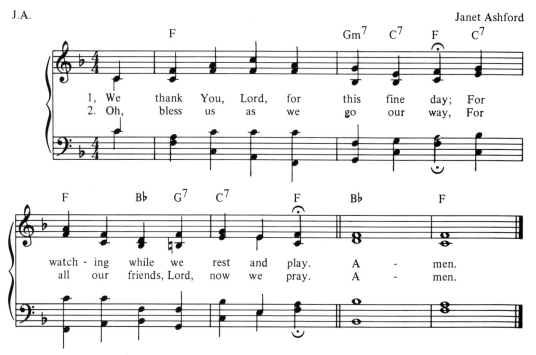

1. We thank You, Lord, for this fine day; For
2. Oh, bless us as we go our way, For

watch-ing while we rest and play. A - men.
all our friends, Lord, now we pray. A - men.

GOOD MORNING TO YOU

M.A.

Mildred Adair

1. Good morn-ing to you, Good morn-ing to you, How are you to - day?_ Good
2. We're glad to see you, We're glad to see you, On this ho - ly day._ We're

morn-ing to you, Good morn-ing to you, This hap-py ho - ly day._____
glad to see you, We're glad to see you, This hap-py ho - ly* day._____

(*Christmas, or any special day may be used.)

WE'LL SAY GOOD-BY

M.A.

Mildred Adair

We'll say "Good-by" to each oth - er, Then bow our heads in prayer,_

"Je - sus, bless us through the week, And keep us in Your care._ A - men."

BIBLE STORY TIME

D.E.

Dana Eynon
Arr. by Alice Koerner

1. Hear the chime? It is Bi - ble sto-ry time.
2. Hear the chime? It is sing - a - sto-ry time.

Time to lis - ten to God's Word, To re - mem - ber what we've heard.
Time to sing a - bout God's Word, Use our voic - es for the Lord.

Hear the chime? It's Bi - ble sto - ry time.
Hear the chime? It's sing - a - sto - ry time.

PUT THE TOYS AWAY

S. T.

Sylvia Tester

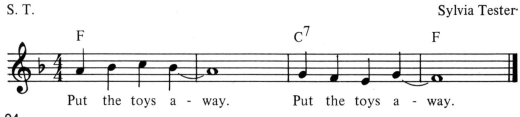

Put the toys a - way. Put the toys a - way.

94

IT'S TIME TO WORSHIP

A. K.

Alice Koerner

1. It's time to stop our play - ing And put our toys a - way. It's
2. It's time to sit to - geth - er, It's time to sing and pray. It's

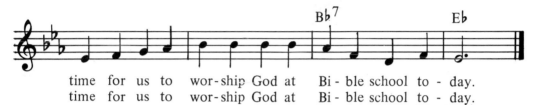

time for us to wor - ship God at Bi - ble school to - day.
time for us to wor - ship God at Bi - ble school to - day.

Substitutions may be made for the first stanza. "It's time to stop our looking and put our books away." "It's time to stop our building and put our blocks away."

HEAR THE CLOCK

Agnes Leckie Mason
Arr. by Phyllis Brown Ohanian

1. Tick, tock, hear the clock, What is that it's say - ing?
2. Tick, tock, hear the clock, What is that it's say - ing?
3. Tick, tock, hear the clock, What is that it's say - ing?
4. Tick, tock, hear the clock, What is that it's say - ing?

"Time to go to Sun-day school." That is what it's say - ing.
"Time to sing a hap - py song." That is what it's say - ing.
"Time to say a qui - et pray'r." That is what it's say - ing.
"Time to hear a sto - ry now." That is what it's say - ing.

INDEX

The numbers after the titles of the songs indicate the approximate ages for which the songs are best suited.